Getting To Know...

Nature's Children

CANADA GEESE

Judy Ross

GROLIER
BOOKS

Facts in Brief

Classification of the Canada Goose

Class: *Aves* (birds)
Order: *Anseriformes* (duck-shaped waterfowl)
Family: *Antidae* (surface duck family)
Genus: *Branta*
Species: *Branta canadensis*

World distribution. Native to North America, but has been introduced to Europe; found seasonally from the Arctic Ocean to Mexico.

Habitat. Marshy areas, ponds, streams, lake shallows.

Distinctive physical characteristics. Broad white band across throat and cheeks; black head, neck, legs, and feet.

Habits. Pairs for life; group migration in "V" formation to South for winter; well-developed communication signals.

Diet. Water plants, grasses, grain, insects.

Edited by: Elizabeth Grace Zuraw
Design/Photo Editor: Nancy Norton
Photo Rights: Ivy Images

ISBN: 0-7172-8725-4

Have you ever wondered . . .

Have you ever been on a "wild goose chase"? That's when you run around chasing after something and never find it. The expression comes from pioneer days when settlers tried to catch a goose to eat. Geese are pretty clever and swift, so often the hunters would come home empty-handed after a long "wild goose chase."

When you think of a goose you may also think of the pictures of Mother Goose in your favorite book of nursery rhymes. The Canada Goose looks quite different. It has a plump gray body and a black neck and head with white patches on its cheeks. (And, of course, it doesn't wear a Mother Goose bonnet!) It does have a very long neck that can twist around in all directions. If you ever see a gooseneck lamp, you'll know where that name came from.

Most people see Canada Geese only when the birds fly overhead honking loudly. Now let's take a closer look at these beautiful creatures.

A male Canada Goose proudly displays his handsome markings.

Splish, Splash!

Do you like taking baths? If you do, you have
something in common with Canada Geese.
Even baby geese enjoy bathtime. They plop
into the water with their parents on a hot
summer day and splash and roll about.
Sometimes one will even do a back flip,
turning over completely to wash its back.

After the bath, the young geese dry off in
the sunshine. But before long they're back
in the water again, poking their heads below
the surface in search of tasty water plants.
Like most young birds, baby geese have
BIG appetites.

*When not bobbing like little corks on the
water, baby geese can most likely be found
enjoying a snack along the water's edge.*

Waterfowl Cousins

Geese are related to ducks and swans. They are all part of a family of birds known as *waterfowl,* or birds that swim. Waterfowl are alike in many ways. They all have short legs and tails, and strong necks and wings.

Most waterfowl *migrate*—twice a year, they fly between feeding grounds in the North and nesting grounds in the South. Their bodies are streamlined for the long distances they fly between their two homes.

If you look at the feet of any waterfowl, you'll see that they're *webbed*—the toes are joined together by flaps of skin. The webbed feet may remind you of rubber swimming flippers. They help the birds swim and dive.

Many birds nest in trees, but ducks, swans, and geese build their nests on the ground. And each year, soon after their eggs have *hatched,* or produced young, all of these birds lose their flight feathers. For a short time, while their new feathers grow in, they cannot fly. If their nests were in trees, they would not be able to get to their young.

Opposite page:
Thanks to its large webbed feet, a Canada Goose has no trouble performing this balancing act.

Big Goose, Little Goose

There are several different types of Canada Geese, but they all have a black head and white patches on their cheeks. You can tell the different types apart by their size, voice, and color. The biggest types of Canada Geese may weigh as much as a small child. They have deep voices and their necks are long. The smaller types have shorter necks, higher voices, and may weigh only as much as a cat.

Each type of Canada Goose has its own special *habitat,* or area in which it lives. For example, some types prefer marshy coastal areas, while others live in the tundra of northern Canada. A *tundra* is the flat, treeless area of the Arctic. And wherever you travel in central and western Canada, you'll probably find at least one type of Canada Goose.

You may be surprised to learn that not all Canada Geese live in Canada. Some types live in the northern United States.

The fine neck feathers of these giant honkers glisten like satin in the bright sunlight.

A Gorgeous Goose

It's difficult to tell a male goose, called a *gander,* from a female goose, but the female tends to be slightly smaller than the male. Both have gleaming feather coats. As they strut about, they almost seem to enjoy showing off their feathers, and they spend a lot of time taking care of them. This is called *preening,* and geese do it every day.

Part of preening is oiling the feathers. With its bill, the goose collects oil from a gland under its tail. A *gland* is a part of an animal's body that makes and gives out a substance. The goose then spreads this oil over all of its feathers. The oil keeps the feathers from drying out and breaking. Most important, this oil helps the goose's coat shed water while it's swimming or in the rain.

Though these Canada Geese appear to be dancing, they actually are preening.

Fantastic Feathers

The goose's handsome coat is made of several kinds of feathers. On the edge of the wings are long, strong flight feathers. Covering its back are feathers that shed water very well and keep the goose's body dry.

Underneath these outer feathers are small fluffy feathers called *down*. They don't have a *shaft*—the hard part down the middle—and so they're very soft. The down feathers keep the goose warm in chilly weather by trapping warm air next to the body. If you've ever slept in a down sleeping bag, you know how cozy that can be.

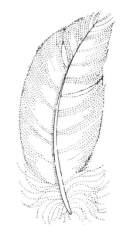

Outer feather

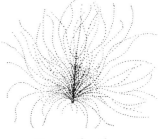

Down feather

A Canada Goose's black flight feathers are replaced each year.

Powerful Wings

A Canada Goose flies at a speed of about 40 miles (65 kilometers) an hour. That's faster than a car travels on a city street. And when it's on a long flight, a goose can fly as high in the sky as some airplanes go.

A goose doesn't use its wings only for flying. When it is running it keeps its wings stretched out for balance. By doing this it can move along at an amazing speed. Its wings are powerful, too, and can be used as weapons when the goose needs to protect itself or its young.

When being chased, a Canada Goose can fly at speeds of up to 60 miles (96 kilometers) an hour.

Bottoms Up

A goose eats about half a pound (one-quarter kilogram) of food a day. It likes grass, grains, berries, corn, and other wild plants.

It uses its long neck to search for food underwater. Like its duck cousins, the goose looks as if it's standing on its head when it's looking for food underwater. All you can see is its white rump sticking up.

When a goose scoops up underwater plants, it also gets a mouthful of water. Little tooth-like spikes around its bill let the water drain out. The tip of a goose's bill is very sensitive to touch. It's used for feeling around under-water for food, as well as for spreading oil on its feathers.

As the geese fly south for the winter, they often stop at a corn or grain field to eat the stubble and plants left over from the harvest. Sometimes they chase after insects in the field. A juicy bug is a great treat for a goose.

Canada Geese feed on water plants in lakes and ponds.

Super Senses

Many animals would like to catch a goose for dinner, so a goose needs to see and hear well in order to stay alive. If you were to sneak up on a *flock,* or large group, of geese, you would soon discover just how good geese's hearing is. At the first crack of a twig or rustle of leaves, the flock would fly off.

No one has yet been able to measure how sharp a goose's eyesight is, but scientists think it's probably very good. Sometimes a goose on the ground will look up into the sky and start calling. The sky looks empty, but in a few minutes a flock of geese will appear. The goose has seen them long before we could.

A goose's eyes are on the sides of its head, so it has to turn its head to see objects in front of it.

Gabby Goose

If you've ever heard a flock of Canada Geese flying overhead and honking, you probably remember the remarkable sound. The Canada Goose is one of the loudest birds around.

The Cree Indians call Canada Geese "the hounds of heaven" because their honking sounds like the barking of hound dogs. Some scientists believe geese stay together in their flocks by "talking" to each other all the time.

Geese make different sounds at different times. The honk is usually heard when they're flying. Special *vocal chords,* the part of the body that produces sound, and a very long neck enable geese to make this unusual honking sound.

If you meet a Canada Goose on the ground, the sound to watch out for is a hiss. A hissing goose extends its neck, opens its mouth wide, and spreads its powerful wings. It's trying to look dangerous—and it is. Be sure to give a hissing goose lots of room!

Migration Mysteries

In the fall, Canada Geese migrate south to warmer climates and head back north in the spring. How do all those geese find their way? No one knows for sure.

Some scientists believe that geese use the moon, sun, and stars to guide them. Others believe that geese sense and are guided by the direction of the Earth's magnetic field. Only one thing is certain: millions of Canada Geese somehow do manage to find their way south every fall and back north every spring.

Canada Geese often fly in formation—in a big V shape, or sometimes in a long line, like a loose string of beads.

At the front of the V is the lead goose. From time to time another goose takes over so that one goose doesn't get too tired. The lead goose is "breaking trail" through the air just as you might break a trail through the snow. This makes flying easier for the geese following behind.

Opposite page: Geese are not the only birds that fly in formation. Ducks and pelicans do, too. But you can always tell geese by their loud honks. The other birds fly silently.

Highways in the Sky

Do you have a special route that you always follow to get from your house to a friend's? Canada Geese have such favorite routes when they migrate. Although some geese can be seen migrating over most parts of the United States, they often use one of four main "highways" in the sky, called *flyways*. These flyways go from northern Canada to the coast of the Gulf of Mexico.

The four flyways are: the Atlantic, and the Pacific, which follow the coasts; the Mississippi, which follows the river; and the Central, which follows the Rocky Mountains. All four have areas of water and food where the geese stop year after year.

As many as a hundred geese may fly south together in a flock. They often fly for many hours without stopping. They land only when they're tired or hungry—or when the weather is bad.

Flocks of migrating geese fill the sky each spring and fall.

A Dangerous Trip

During the long flight south, the flock faces many dangers. Rain and hailstones slow them down, and fall is hunting season. All along the route hunters wait for the geese to pass by. With all these dangers, many of the geese never make it.

There are some places along the routes where hunting is not allowed. These marshy areas have many lakes and plenty of food for the tired and hungry geese. The geese seem to know where these safe spots are and land on them every year.

Winter Homes

By the time the geese reach their winter home in the South, they've lost weight because of all the flying they have done. They'll spend most of the winter resting and putting on weight. The geese must build up a good layer of fat to be ready for the long flight north in the spring.

Opposite page: *This goose has wandered off by itself, but when a flock of geese has come together, especially on the ground, the group is called a gaggle.*

Choosing a Mate

Two- and three-year-old geese choose mates while they're in the South for the winter. Since Canada Geese mate for life, older geese already have partners. An older goose chooses a new mate only if its mate has died.

Opposite page: *Out-honked and out-hissed, this unwelcome gander will have to look elsewhere for a mate.*

Scientists have observed a gander spend as much as three days looking over a group of females before deciding which one to pursue. Then he tries to get her away from the flock. But it's the female who makes the final choice. If she isn't interested, she ignores her pursuer, or tries to shoo him away.

Sometimes, if two ganders have their eye on the same female, they will fight. The angry ganders stretch their necks straight out like spears and charge, hissing loudly and flapping their wings. If one doesn't back off, they may hit each other with the bony edges of their wings and snap at each other with their bills.

When the fighting is over and the female has chosen her mate, the goose pair stretch their necks up and down and honk loudly. From now on, they will always be together.

Back Home To Nest

Opposite page:
*A raised nest
site gives the
protective goose
mother an
excellent view
of the marsh.*

Late in March, the days grow longer and the goose and the gander grow restless. It's time for them to go back to the place where they themselves were born, and to *mate,* or come together to produce young.

Their first job when they arrive back at their summer home is to choose a place to make a nest. They choose the place very carefully. The goose and the gander mate in the water and usually nest near the water, too. The favorite spots are marshy places or small islands in a lake or pond. But sometimes a pair builds a nest away from a lake, in a wet, spongy area called a *bog.*

Although geese are friendly birds and travel together in big flocks, the mother and father goose seem to like to be alone when they're nesting. They prefer not to have geese living right next door. But they don't seem to mind if a duck family moves into the neighborhood!

Sometimes, two pairs of geese fight over a nesting area. Both pairs honk and hiss until one leaves to find another nesting spot.

Getting to Work

The female goose builds the nest. She pulls together a pile of twigs and marsh grasses with her bill. Then she makes a nice rounded hole in the top of the pile with her body. Finally she plucks soft, warm down feathers from her chest to make a cozy lining for the nest.

The mother goose usually lays between three and eight creamy-white eggs. After each egg is laid, she pulls more feathers from her chest until she has a bare spot on her skin. She then presses this bare skin against the eggs to keep them warm. Periodically, she turns the eggs over with her bill to keep the temperature of the eggs even.

Within a month of being laid, these goose eggs will produce four fluffy babies.

Waiting—and Watching

For 25 to 30 days, the mother goose sits on her eggs. A goose father doesn't take turns on the nest as some bird fathers do. Instead, he stands guard, making sure no egg-stealers get near the nest. If he senses danger he flies into the air, honking loudly to frighten the intruder. Sometimes he may even attack, hissing, biting, and flapping his wings ferociously. Although there are many animals that might like to have a tasty goose egg for dinner, few will take on this angry parent.

The female doesn't leave the nest. Instead, she crouches low over it so that she and her nest will not be seen by *predators,* animals that hunt other animals for food.

Happy Hatchday

When the eggs are ready to hatch, little peeps, cheeps, and tap-tapping sounds come from inside the eggs. This is the way a baby goose, called a *gosling* (GAHZ-ling), says, "I'm ready to come out now!"

Egg tooth on a gosling's bill

Each gosling has a special, hard *egg tooth* on the top of its bill to help chip through its shell. First a small hole appears in the shell, followed by a crack. Breaking out of its shell is very hard work for a gosling, but the mother and father just stand by watching. The little gosling inside the egg might be hurt if the mother or father poked at the egg from the outside. Finally, a tiny bill pokes out through the shell. Then the gosling's head appears, with its eyes blinking at the bright new world.

After the wet little body is out of the shell, the gosling lies down to rest while its feathers dry. Within 24 hours, all its brothers and sisters will hatch, too. The newly hatched family is called a *clutch* of geese.

Overleaf:
A mother goose almost never leaves the nest— and the father never sits on it. His responsibility is to defend it, a job he performs fiercely.

Are You My Mother?

Unlike many other animal babies, a gosling doesn't know who its parents are when it is first born. It thinks that the first animal it sees is its parent. If a horse is the first animal a gosling sees after hatching, it will think that the horse is its parent! This is why the goose parents stay close to the nest. They are making sure that their babies see them first and will know them as their parents. *Imprinting* is the name given to the experience of a newborn of some animals to recognize the first object it sees as its parent.

Raring to Go

Within hours, the goslings leave the nest. And once they do, they never return to it.

The goslings' fluffy little bodies are an olive-yellow color. The babies change and grow quickly. Sometimes they double their weight in the first week of life. By the time they're two weeks old, the goslings turn gray, and their soft down begins to be covered by feathers. In six weeks they have black feathers, and their white cheek patches begin to show.

Growing Up

Opposite page:
Swimming is one of the first and most important lessons a gosling must learn. And the babies have usually mastered the skill by the time they're just a few days old.

One of the first lessons a gosling must learn is how to swim. To do that, it has to get to the water. Most of the time the nest is close by and the goslings don't have to go very far. But sometimes, if a nest is far from water, the goose family may have to walk to it. The family travels single file in a straight line. The mother leads the way, the goslings follow her, and the father brings up the rear. The little balls of fluff march behind their mother, crossing busy roads, and climbing up and down over rocks, logs, and hills—all to get to water.

During the summer months, the goslings eat and grow. They learn by copying what their parents do. They learn what food to look for and where to find it. They practice tipping upside down to find food underwater. And they learn the danger signs—the sign of a fox in the grass or the sight of a hawk circling in the sky. Even a day-old gosling is able to get away from danger by diving and swimming underwater for more than 30 feet (10 meters).

Opposite page:
*Tall grasses
help provide
necessary cover
for grounded
goose families
until their flight
feathers grow in.*

Grounded!

Every year at the same time, when the goslings are half grown, the mother and father lose the big feathers on their wings and tail. Losing one set of feathers and growing another is called *molting*. During this time, the geese cannot fly, but they're not helpless. They still run across the water flapping their wings to speed them along.

Learning to Fly

By the time the parents' new feathers have grown in, the goslings are ready to learn to fly. The babies seem to know how to fly. They don't need much teaching. Their first flights are short ones, but soon they follow their parents to new feeding grounds.

By the time the young Canada Geese are eight weeks old, they're hard to tell apart from their parents because they are fully grown. They may now be 25 times bigger than they were at birth. If people grew that fast, a two-month old baby would weigh as much as a grown man!

Summer's End

At the end of summer, the goose family leaves the nesting area and moves to a new feeding ground. There they are joined by other goose families all looking for food.

When the flock is feeding there is one goose, called a *sentinel,* who stands guard. The others munch happily on marsh grasses and pond weeds. The sentinel often finds a high spot of land where it can look all around, bending its flexible neck in all directions. If the sentinel senses danger, it honks loudly to warn the others.

Time To Go South Again

As summer turns to fall, the weather turns colder and the grasses and weeds dry out and die. Once again, the geese become restless. The shorter days warn them that winter is coming. They start to gather in large groups for the long flight south to their winter home. When you hear their honks and see their V-formation in the sky, you, too, will know that winter is coming.

Words To Know

Bog   An area with wet spongy ground.

Clutch   Eggs laid by a bird, and the babies that hatch from them.

Down   Very soft, fluffy feathers.

Egg tooth   A tooth-like point on the tip of a baby goose's bill used to help it crack out of its shell.

Flock   A large group of birds that lives and feeds together.

Flyways   Special routes that birds use on their migrations.

Gaggle   A flock of geese, especially on the ground.

Gander   Male goose.

Gland   Animal body part that makes and gives out a substance.

Goslings   Young geese.

Habitat   The area in which an animal or plant naturally lives.

Hatch   To break out of an egg.

Imprinting   The name given to the experience of some animals in which a newborn recognizes the first animal it sees as its parent.

Mate   To come together to produce young.

Migrate   To move from one place to another.

Molt   To lose one set of feathers and grow another.

Predator   An animal that hunts other animals for food.

Preening   Cleaning, smoothing, and oiling the feathers.

Sentinel   A look-out bird that guards a feeding flock.

Shaft   The hard stem down the middle of a feather.

Tundra   Flat land in the Arctic where no trees grow.

Waterfowl   Birds that swim.

Webbed feet   Feet with toes joined together by flaps of skin.

Index

PHOTO CREDITS
Cover: Robert McCaw, *Ivy Images*. **Interiors:** Bill Ivy, 4, 8, 11, 13, 14, 17, 21, 22, 29, 30, 41, 43.
/*Visuals Unlimited:* Glenn M. Oliver, 7; William J. Weber, 18; Tom Edwards, 24. /*Maslowski Photo*, 26. /*Ivy Images:* Robert McCaw, 33. /*Network Stock Photo File:* Barry Griffiths, 34, 45.

Getting To Know...

Nature's Children

GRIZZLY BEARS

Caroline Greenland

GROLIER
BOOKS

Facts in Brief

Classification of the Grizzly Bear

Class:	*Mammalia* (mammals)
Order:	*Carnivora* (meat-eaters)
Family:	*Ursidae* (bear family)
Genus:	*Urus*
Species:	*Ursus arctos* (Brown Bear)
Subspecies:	*Ursus arctos horribilis* (Grizzly Bear)

World distribution. Exclusive to North America; closely related to the European Brown Bear, which lives in Europe and Asia.

Habitat. Seem to prefer open meadows and river valleys but may also be found in forests and lower mountain slopes.

Distinctive physical characteristics. Very large; thick, gray-flecked fur, especially long around neck; long, curved claws.

Habits. Solitary; usually establishes territory, marking it by clawing trees; winters in den but is not a true hibernator.

Diet. Will eat whatever is available—roots, leafy plants, berries, small animals, fish.

Edited by: Elizabeth Grace Zuraw
Design/Photo Editor: Nancy Norton
Photo Rights: Ivy Images

ISBN: 0-7172-8726-2

Have you ever wondered . . .

How did the Grizzly Bear get its name? It may be because of the color of its coat. The tips of the fur are *grizzled,* or flecked with gray. Or it may be because the Grizzly Bear is thought to be fierce. Something that is terrible or frightening is often described as *grisly.*

Whatever the origin of its name, the Grizzly does have a bad reputation. Even though Grizzlies are intelligent and shy, many people think of them as ferocious and dangerous. Usually, the only Grizzlies that will attack a person are a mother bear protecting her cubs or a Grizzly that is cornered or startled.

In those rare cases where a Grizzly does attack, it will fight with courage and great strength. But most of the time Grizzlies don't look for trouble.

Grizzlies can look as fuzzy and cuddly as a teddy bear, but this is one bear you don't want to hug.

Meet a Grizzly Bear Cub

Fishing can be pretty hard work for a Grizzly Bear cub. There are so many delicious salmon swimming along—and they're just out of reach. But maybe if the cub stretches its paw out just a little more…and then leans over just a little bit and…SPLASH!

But you needn't worry. All Grizzly cubs know how to swim. Besides, if this cub doesn't manage to catch a fish soon, its mother will catch one for her little one. Like all Grizzly babies, this cub will sit nervously on the river-bank, straining to keep its mother in sight while she fishes. But as soon as she returns with a fish, the cub will be happy and playful again, knowing its protector is close by.

If you would like to know more about this appealing little creature—and big Grizzly Bears, too—read on.

Grizzly cubs quickly learn not to disobey their mother. That's because she not only will scold them but will probably cuff them with her paw.

The Bear Facts

The Grizzly Bear is one of the largest animals in North America. Male Grizzlies, called *boars,* are usually larger than females, or *sows.* Most boars weigh about 700 pounds (320 kilograms). Some may weigh as much as seven grown men! Male Grizzlies keep on growing throughout their lives, so the older they get, the bigger they are.

Grizzlies often look bigger than they really are because of their long, thick fur. The hair around a Grizzly's neck is especially long. It looks like a ruff or cape and flops around as the bear runs.

Grizzly Bears may be any color, from creamy yellow to nearly black. But no matter what the color, the fur is flecked with gray, giving it the grizzled look.

Bears growl, whine, cry, and bawl. And when they're surprised, they say something that sounds like "whooosh."

9

Bear Country

There are bears in many countries, but you'll find the Grizzly Bear only in North America. Some Grizzlies live in Mexico, but most are in the northwestern United States, western Canada, and Alaska.

Grizzly Bears seem to prefer living in open meadows or river valleys. But they also live in forests at the bottom of mountains. Some may even wander into the treeless wilderness areas of the North.

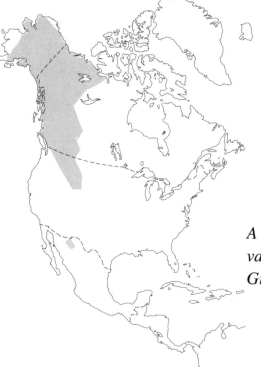

Where Grizzly Bears live in North America

A Grizzly looks out over a deep river valley, one of the types of places that Grizzlies prefer to live in.

Bear Relatives

Grizzlies are related to Polar Bears and Black Bears. Their closest cousins, however, are the Alaskan Brown Bear and the European Brown Bear, which lives in Europe and Asia.

Black Bear

All of these bears have certain things in common. They eat meat as well as plants, and they have two kinds of teeth to chew food. They walk flat on their feet, and their front feet are slightly pigeon-toed. This makes a bear look clumsy and slow when it walks.

Grizzly Bear

Polar Bear

Grizzlies belong to a group of bears called Big Brown Bears. Alaskan Brown Bears, such as the one shown here, look a lot like the Grizzly but are even bigger. All Brown Bears have a hump on the shoulders, just behind the neck—a quick and easy way to identify them.

13

Stay Out

Most Grizzly Bears have their own *territory,* an area where an animal lives and spends most of its time. For a Grizzly, this piece of land may be as large as 6 square miles (16 square kilometers). If food is scarce, the Grizzly's territory may be even bigger.

To let other bears know that a territory is already taken, a Grizzly leaves long claw marks on trees as high up as it can reach. Any bear who ignores these "stay out" signs may be in for a fight.

Grizzly Bears can grow to a height of 8 feet (2.4 meters). They stand up to check out their surroundings and to scare enemies away. Native Americans called Grizzlies "the beasts that walk like people." Looking at this picture, it's easy to see why.

Super Sniffer and Sharp Ears

Look at the Grizzly Bear's long snout. Do you think that it has a keen sense of smell? If you said "yes," you're right. The Grizzly uses its sensitive nose to search for food and to avoid other animals. It needs such a good nose for many reasons. For one thing, it can't see very well. For another, the Grizzly is most active from dusk to dawn, when eyesight is not all that useful.

Like most animals that are *nocturnal,* or active in the dark, the Grizzly has excellent hearing in addition to a good sense of smell. Those furry, rounded ears can even pick up the sound of a twig cracking far away.

Grizzlies have a keen sense of smell and can sniff out dinner from a long way off.

On the Move

You may think that a Grizzly Bear looks pretty clumsy as it lumbers along. And with its big shoulders hunched over and its head held low and swinging back and forth, it may look slow, too. But for short distances, a Grizzly Bear can run about as fast as a horse.

The Grizzly walks and runs on its whole foot just as people do. Many other animals, such as horses, deer, and dogs, walk on their toes. Being flat-footed means the Grizzly can stand upright and even take a few steps on its hind legs. This is useful when its curiosity is aroused. By standing as tall as possible, it can pick up interesting smells with its super nose.

Grizzly Bear tracks

Grizzlies are powerful, fearless, aggressive, and unpredictable—good reasons for people and other animals to avoid them.

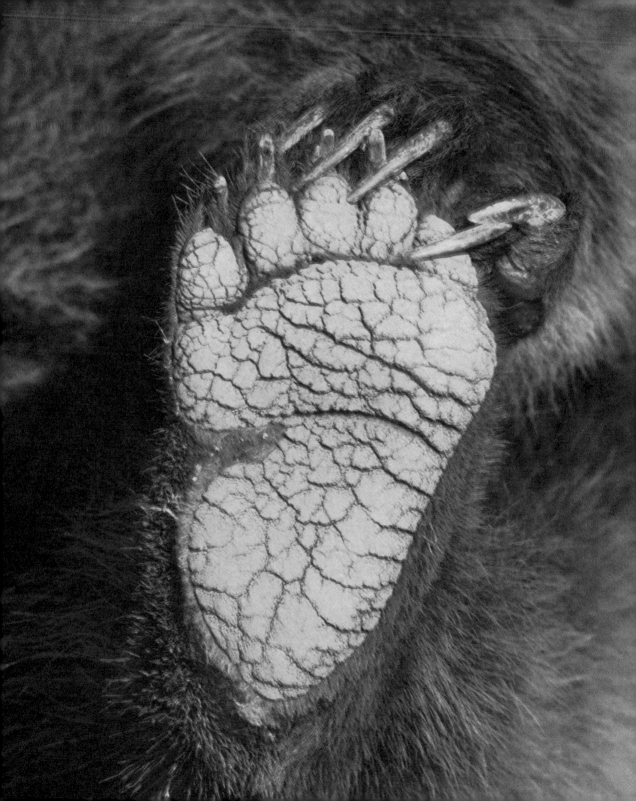

Bear Feet

A Grizzly Bear has five toes on each foot, and every toe has a long curved claw that is about the length of a new crayon. These claws help the bear dig roots and catch fish. After a summer of digging, the bear's claws get worn down. But they grow back over the winter to full length, ready for a new season of digging.

You can tell how old a Grizzly is just by looking at its claws. A young Grizzly's claws are usually black or very dark brown with light tips. But as the bear grows older, its claws get lighter in color. Some very old bears have pure white claws.

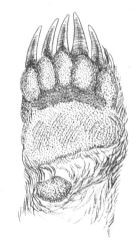

Grizzly's front foot

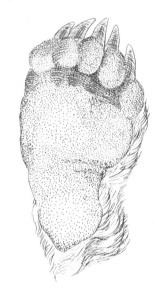

Grizzly's back foot

A bear's long, curved claws can always be seen because, unlike those of a cat, they have no covering and can't be drawn in.

21

What an Appetite!

In the wild, Grizzlies eat just about anything that's available—young plants, roots, grasses, berries, insects, and fish. The Grizzly eats any meat that it finds, too. Sometimes it goes after *prey,* animals hunted by other animals for food.

A Grizzly uses its long claws to dig out mice, Ground Squirrels, and marmots from their underground homes. It also hunts elk, moose, and Mountain Sheep.

If a Grizzly has more meat than it can eat at one sitting, it drags off the leftovers and hides them from other hungry animals by covering them with branches. In this way, the Grizzly can have meal after meal by returning to the hiding place.

Grizzlies usually sleep during the day and feed in the evening and at night. But if food is scarce, a Grizzly may hunt for food during the day, too.

A Bad Habit

Have you ever visited the local dump while you were out camping or at a cottage? You probably weren't the only visitor. Many bears, including Grizzlies, feast on food left behind by people.

Food that it finds in the wild is much better for a Grizzly than leftover human food. Our leftovers contain too much sugar. If a Grizzly eats too much of it, it might get cavities. And there is nothing more miserable than a bear with a sore tooth.

Overleaf:
Grizzlies most often are loners, but will gather in large numbers at a good feeding spot. A river flowing with salmon is sure to attract many Grizzlies.

Grizzlies often rummage around campsites and dumps in search of leftover human food.

Expert Fishers

In the summer, Grizzlies on the west coast crowd along riverbanks to feast on their favorite food, salmon. As the salmon swim upriver to lay their eggs, the bears prepare for a feast. The strongest bears make sure they get the best fishing spots, and they defend these places with growls and threatening head swings if another bear comes too near. The youngest bears have to make do with the spots that are left over.

A Grizzly has two ways of catching fish. It can stand in the water and swiftly scoop out a salmon with its paw. This fish dinner is then carried to the side of the river and eaten whole. Or the bear can stay on the riverbank watching carefully. The instant a salmon happens to swim by—SPLASH!—in goes the hungry Grizzly after it.

Most Grizzlies can catch between two and four fish per hour.

Open Wide!

Because of its varied diet, a Grizzly bear needs teeth that can chew a lot of different foods. Grizzly *molars,* the flat teeth at the back of the mouth, are good for grinding plant stems and roots. A Grizzly's front teeth are large and pointed. They're good for tearing into prey.

A Grizzly has 42 teeth, including the powerful *canines,* the long, pointed, front teeth on each side of the jaw. Old bears have especially long canines because bear teeth continue to grow throughout the animal's life.

Grizzlies are omnivores, they eat both meat and plants. This bear's awesome teeth can easily handle all kinds of food.

Mating Season

A Grizzly Bear rarely has anything to do with another Grizzly—except during *mating season,* the time of year during which animals come together to produce young. A female mates with a male every other year in June and July. Then the two Grizzlies go their separate ways. When the cubs are born the next winter, the mother Grizzly raises them on her own.

Usually unfriendly with one another, Grizzlies stay together during mating season. A male and female become quite playful, rubbing noses when they're ready to mate. They may also give each other a gentle bear hug.

Cold Weather Signals

If you were to observe a Grizzly Bear closely, you'd be able to tell when the cold weather was about to arrive. First you would look at the Grizzly's fur. As the days get colder, the Grizzly grows an extra-thick fur coat. This coat is actually two coats in one. The inner coat, the thick short *underfur,* traps body-warmed air next to the Grizzly's skin. The outer coat, made of long *guard hairs,* helps shed rain or snow that might chill the bear.

Next you would watch how much the Grizzly eats. In the fall, it eats as much food as it can find. The bear isn't unusually hungry; it's just trying to put on weight. The fatter the bear is, the better its chance of surviving a long cold winter with little or no food.

And you will know for sure that winter is very near when the Grizzly starts searching for a *den,* a shelter used as a home by an animal.

In the fall, in order to get fattened up enough to survive the cold winter ahead, a Grizzly may eat 80 to 90 pounds (36 to 40.5 kilograms) of food a day.

Digging in

By mid-November food becomes scarce, so the Grizzly starts to search for a place to sleep away the winter. Caves, hollow logs, or shelters under fallen trees make the best dens.

If a Grizzly can't find a den, it must make one for itself. It uses its long claws to dig a hole, often under a rock on a steep hill. When the Grizzly has dug a bear-size hole, it lines the den with dead leaves, branches, and grass. Then it climbs in and waits for snow to cover the den entrance. The snow helps to keep the bear's den hidden from other animals until spring.

It may be cold outside, but a Grizzly is cozy when it tucks itself into its den. A hole dug in a hillside makes a comfortable winter home.

A Long Sleep

During the winter, some animals *hibernate,* they go into a kind of heavy sleep in which their breathing and heart rate slow, and their body temperature drops. Although the Grizzly sleeps away most of the winter, its long sleep isn't true hibernation. The bear's breathing rate and body temperature change very little, and it may occasionally wake up during the winter. It may even move around outside the den if the weather is mild. True hibernators, such as Ground Squirrels, do not wake up at all until spring arrives. But whether it's true hibernation or not, Grizzlies spend the winter months in their snug dens.

A Grizzly occasionally leaves its den during the winter, especially if the weather turns mild.

Baby Bears

Opposite page:
A Grizzly mother and cub stay together for one or two years.

Many animal babies are born in the spring, but not Grizzly cubs. They're born in mid-winter. One of the first sounds the newborns hear is the winter wind howling outside the den. But the kitten-size Grizzly cubs don't have to worry about getting cold. They snuggle up close to their mother's warm, furry body to stay warm.

As the winter winds blow and the snow flies, the cubs *nurse,* drink milk from their mother's body. Usually two cubs are born at the same time, but the number can vary from one to four. The cubs weigh at most one pound (about half a kilogram) at birth, and their eyes don't open until they're about a month old. But doing nothing besides sleeping and drinking their mother's rich milk, the cubs grow quickly. In about two months, they weigh around 20 pounds (9 kilograms). By then the den is getting crowded—and it's spring, time for the bear family to go outside.

Bear School

When spring arrives, the Grizzly cubs come rolling out of their den looking like fat, furry balls. They're frisky and ready to play—but their mother has other ideas. It's time for bear school. The cubs have to learn the lessons they need in order to survive.

The young bears stay with their mother for one or two years. By watching her, the cubs learn how to hunt and how to tell which foods are good to eat and which ones must be avoided. And they learn which animals are dangerous to young cubs.

Adult Grizzlies have few enemies. Though they're peaceful animals, when they do need to defend themselves, one blow from their powerful front paw can kill even a large enemy. But cubs are in danger from *predators,* animals that hunt other animals for food. Sometimes, even adult male Grizzlies attack Grizzly cubs.

Opposite page:
A young Grizzly cub stays close on its mother's heels even if that means wading into a stream behind her.

43

A Good Mother

The Grizzly is a good mother. She protects her cubs and can be quite fierce if she thinks they are in danger. She's a good teacher, too. Most of the time she is patient and kind. But sometimes she'll cuff the cubs if they're doing something that could be dangerous.

When they first leave the den, the Grizzly cubs stay close on their mother's heels. But by the end of their first summer, their mother starts letting them go off together to explore on their own.

Grizzlies, even cubs, like to live in open areas rather than in forests.

Growing Up

During the next winter, the cubs stay with their mother and share a den with her. But come spring, the female is ready to mate again, and the youngsters are shooed away— sometimes not too gently. The sow will have plenty to do looking after her new cubs without having to worry about the two-year-olds as well.

The young bears then rely on each other to stay out of danger. The next winter they may den together, but in the spring they'll separate, each going its own way. If they remember everything their mother has taught them, they can live for as long as 25 years as magnificent Grizzlies in the wild.

Words To Know

Boar   Male bear.

Den   An animal home or shelter.

Guard hairs   Long coarse hairs that make up the outer layer of a Grizzly's coat.

Hibernation   A kind of heavy sleep that some animals take in the winter, during which their breathing and heart rates slow, and their body temperature drops.

Mate   To come together to produce young.

Mating season   The time of year when animals mate.

Molars   Back teeth that are suited for grinding food.

Nocturnal   Active mainly at night.

Nurse   To drink milk from a mother's body.

Omnivores   Animals that eat both plants and meat.

Predator   An animal that hunts other animals for food.

Prey   An animal hunted by other animals for food.

Sow   Female bear.

Territory   The area that an animal or group of animals lives in and often defends against other animals of the same kind.

Underfur   Thick short hair that traps body-warmed air next to a Grizzly's skin.

Index

PHOTO CREDITS
Cover: Bill Ivy. **Interiors:** *Valan Photos:* Stephen J. Krasemann, 4, 8, 16, 19, 23, 35, 38, 45; Brian Milne, 12, 41, 42. */Canada In Stock / Ivy Images:* Gary Crandall, 7, 28. */Tom Stack & Associates:* John Shaw, 11, 15; Thomas Kitchin, 20. /Wayne Lynch, 24. /Mark Emery, 26-27, 36. /Thomas Kitchin, 31, 32.